Surviving In A Cordless World

Gospel Sermons For Sundays
After Pentecost (Middle Third)
Cycle B

Lawrence H. Craig

CSS Publishing Company, Inc., Lima, Ohio

SURVIVING IN A CORDLESS WORLD

Copyright © 1999 by
CSS Publishing Company, Inc.
Lima, Ohio

All rights reserved. No part of this publication may be reproduced in any manner whatsoever without the prior permission of the publisher, except in the case of brief quotations embodied in critical articles and reviews. Inquiries should be addressed to: Permissions, CSS Publishing Company, Inc., P.O. Box 4503, Lima, Ohio 45802-4503.

Scripture quotations are from the *New Revised Standard Version of the Bible*, copyright 1989 by the Division of Christian Education of the National Council of the Churches of Christ in the USA. Used by permission.

Library of Congress Cataloging-in-Publication Data

Craig, Lawrence H.
    Surviving in a cordless world : Gospel sermons for Sundays after Pentecost (middle third), Cycle B / Lawrence H. Craig.
        p.   cm.
    ISBN 0-7880-1500-1 (pbk. : alk. paper)
    1. Pentecost season Sermons. 2. Bible. N.T. Gospel Sermons. 3. Sermons, American.
I. Title.
BV61.C73   1999
252'.64—dc21
                                                      99-33001
                                                          CIP

This book is available in the following formats, listed by ISBN:
    0-7880-1500-1   Book
    0-7880-1501-X   Disk
    0-7880-1502-8   Sermon Prep

For more information about CSS Publishing Company resources, visit our website at www.csspub.com.

PRINTED IN U.S.A.

This book is dedicated

*In Memory
of*

my mother,

Ruth W. Craig,

*for her many faithful years of unfailing love, support,
inspiration, and guidance to her family*

and

*In Honor and Celebration
of*

our family's first grandchild,

Erica Lynn Craig,

*whose birth and beginning of life's journey brings
continued new joy, meaningfulness, and
reaffirmation of God's presence to our daily lives.*

For an additional sermon by Lawrence Craig, visit our website at www.csspub.com.

Table Of Contents

Foreword — 7

Proper 10
Pentecost 8
Ordinary Time 15 — 9
    Living Between A Rock And A Hard Place
    Mark 6:14-29

Proper 11
Pentecost 9
Ordinary Time 16 — 15
    Surviving In A Cordless World
    Mark 6:30-34, 53-56

Proper 12
Pentecost 10
Ordinary Time 17 — 21
    Pulling Valves And Pushing Fish
    John 6:1-21

Proper 13
Pentecost 11
Ordinary Time 18 — 27
    Beneath Life's Surface Scenes
    John 6:24-35

Proper 14
Pentecost 12
Ordinary Time 19 — 33
    Wearing The 7C6 Label
    John 6:35, 41-51

Proper 15
Pentecost 13
Ordinary Time 20 — 39
    Beyond The Oak Table
    John 6:51-58

Proper 16   **43**
Pentecost 14
Ordinary Time 21
    The Raft Of Passage
    John 6:56-69

Proper 17   **49**
Pentecost 15
Ordinary Time 22
    Hey, Don't Ruin The Bean Pot!
    Mark 7:1-8, 14-15, 21-23

Proper 18   **55**
Pentecost 16
Ordinary Time 23
    Who Are You?
    Mark 7:24-37

Proper 19   **61**
Pentecost 17
Ordinary Time 24
    The Fine Print
    Mark 8:27-38

Proper 20   **67**
Pentecost 18
Ordinary Time 25
    Focus
    Mark 9:30-37

Lectionary Preaching After Pentecost   **71**

Foreword

The doors of the twentieth century close while, simultaneously, the doors to the twenty-first century open wide. The new millennium beckons us to enter. As we cross that threshold, stretching out before us is an exciting world of wonder and challenge we can only begin to imagine.

Who would have believed that in a brief one hundred years, we would go from the Wright brothers' first flight at Kitty Hawk to running shuttles to and from space with such regularity and ease? Who would have believed that the day would come when paper-filled brief cases would become obsolete and be replaced by disk-demanding laptops? Today's world is a very much different place than it was even thirty years ago. The world of cell phones, e-mail, and fax machines has opened our minds to high-tech living, while often closing our hearts to the importance of remaining personally connected with each other and with God.

From the time the umbilical cord is severed, throughout the journey of our lives, until our own deaths we find ourselves struggling to survive in a cordless world. Yet, we are not alone in the journey. The ever-faithful God is always present to us. The lives of other persons are also present to us wherever we find ourselves at any given time along the stations of our lives. These persons teach, encourage, influence, and fashion us into the persons we shall ultimately become.

The following messages were preached to a congregation gathered for worship as God's faithful people. These contemporary messages are the cumulative result of various life-enriching learnings and experiences. They are my gift to others who search in life to discover God's word of strength, receive an inspirational illustration, or seek a harbor of hope for their personal faith journey and for the faith journeys of those to whom they minister. These messages are a mix of stories, events, interactions, and influences of people, all who have contributed to this author's connectedness to God and God's people throughout an ever-unfolding ministry and personal life journey. This author's hope is that these messages become part of the spiritual brick and mortar that assists the readers toward building a more Christ-centered life, thus enabling themselves and others not only to survive in a cordless society, but also to celebrate God's blessings in today's cordless world.

Therefore, it is only appropriate to acknowledge the people behind the preacher, the special persons who have been influential throughout my own faith journey. I am greatly indebted to my family:

My father, Gene, who over the years by his quiet way of wisdom has contributed more to my life by example than he will ever realize.

My wife, Christina, whose continued love, patience, encouragement, and belief in me have been priceless blessings which have immensely contributed to the person I've become.

I remain especially grateful to my two children, Sean and Heather, whose own personal life achievements are the catalyst of inspiration that generates the joy and challenge for me to "keep on keeping on."

A tremendous debt of thanks is owed to Wanda S. Lester, secretary and friend. Her counsel and computer experience, along with tireless hours of patience and time given to interpreting my handwritten hieroglyphics resulted in these messages being properly prepared for publication.

Most important of all is the on-going influence of the living God, a God whose faithful presence continues to do new things in this author's life and, I pray, will be about doing new things in your life as well.

Lawrence H. Craig

Proper 10 • Pentecost 8 • Ordinary Time 15

Living Between A Rock And A Hard Place

Mark 6:14-29

While persons were working on the White Pass Yukon Route Railroad near Skagway, Alaska, on August 3, 1898, a great tragedy occurred. During the blasting of rock to clear a passage for the laying of ties and track, a one hundred-ton granite boulder worked loose from where it had rested. This enormous rock came down upon two railroad workers, burying them between itself and the hard terrain beneath them. Having died instantly, and because of the immensity of the stone, any attempt to recover the men's bodies was not an option. Therefore, a black cross was placed upon the granite boulder to mark the final resting place of these two men. Today that black cross remains and can still be seen on the granite rock at the side of the railroad tracks near Skagway, Alaska. The boulder, with its black cross, has become a memorial to the more than thirty men who lost their lives during the construction of that railroad.

Any event, such as this boulder pinning the two men against a rock and a hard place, which prematurely ends in the loss of human life, is a great tragedy in the eyes of humankind. However, great tragedies are not only limited to persons who suffer physical death. Any event which leads a person to suffer a spiritual death becomes itself a great tragedy, especially in the eyes of the loving God who gives us the gift of life.

The lesson before us describes the senseless and tragic physical death of John the Baptist. Yet, even more tragic and more senseless is what happened to King Herod in this scriptural story.

The two railroad workers' physical lives were abruptly ended, having been caught between a large granite boulder and the hard, rocky terrain beneath them. Herod's spiritual life ended abruptly on his birthday. Herod was celebrating God's precious gift of life when his decisions and actions that day resulted in his spiritual death. Herod's decisions and actions also resulted abruptly in the spiritual death of those around him who were influenced by his poor decisions and examples. Herod was simply trying to live between a rock and a hard place. He was doing what we commonly refer to today as trying to have his cake and eat it too, and on his birthday no less. He was attempting to walk the fence and avoid choosing one side over the other. The end result is that Herod fell away from God. Herod lost the balance that one needs between the physical and spiritual aspects of life.

Revealed in this scriptural story before us is the dichotomy of life. Revealed is life as we morally know it and are challenged by God to live it. Revealed is life lived in absence of a relationship to God. This biblical story began when John the Baptist took a moral stand against Herod, who chose to live immorally. Allow me to share the story with you.

King Herod had engaged in an extramarital affair with Herodias, who was not only the wife of his brother, but also his niece by marriage. Herod kicked his own wife out and married Herodias while she was still his brother's wife. John the Baptist had the courage to take a moral stand. He confronted Herod about his errant ways. John told Herod that his lifestyle was contrary to religious law.

When Herod told Herodias about John's criticism of their relationship, Herodias wanted John killed. Herod dealt with the situation by trying to please himself and please Herodias at the same time.

Herod wanted Herodias in the worst way, but he also feared killing the Baptist, for John was a holy man, one of God, who intrigued Herod with his preaching. Therefore, to keep John alive and please his new wife, Herod spared John the Baptist's life by putting him in prison.

The day came for Herod's birthday. This was a time to party — a time for Herod to impress all his family and subjects. The big extravaganza was held at the palace. Herodias was in her glory. The families, the friends, and the relatives were all invited along with anyone who was someone in the kingdom. The King's court and the leaders of Galilee were present. And what a party it was!

Yet, we continue to find Herod living between that rock and a hard place. During the party the seductive dancing by prostitutes began. Herodias' teenage daughter was there. She decided to dance as well. Instead of appropriately putting a stop to her behavior, Herodias let her go. Herod noticed his guests were very pleased with the young girl's dancing. He could have decided to do what was morally and ethically proper as a parent and stop the child, yet he chose to keep his guests happy and keep his popularity. He sacrificed the young girl's innocence and reputation.

Herod became consumed by it all. When the dance ended, Herod said to the daughter, in front of everyone in attendance, "Ask me for whatever you wish and I will give it" (Mark 6: 22c).

Making matters worse, Herod went a step further. He sealed his comment with a binding oath. Again he said, "Whatever you ask me, I will give you, even half of my kingdom" (Mark 6:23).

Now we find Herod really living between a rock and a hard place. The rock of destruction was pressing heavily upon him and the hard place was beginning to wear on his nerves. Then came the clincher. The daughter, in her teens, couldn't decide what she should ask to have. Corvettes weren't invented yet, neither were stereo sound systems or CD players. Because of Herod and Herodias' position and wealth, the daughter probably had everything anyway. She really believed this was a decision that had to be discussed with Mom. After all, Herod had promised and vowed, in front of all the party guests, to give her anything. Anything she asked! Imagine the scene! The suspense! The drama! The excitement!

The daughter ran to discuss the situation with her mother. A hushed silence, like the calm before a violent storm, moved across the palace, out onto the lawn, and over all of Herod's birthday party guests. The party-goers had heard Herod clearly. They knew their King had backed up his offer with his oath.

Whispers were beginning to be heard from ear to ear, person to person. What would the dancing daughter ask to receive? What would her request be, once she had consulted with Herodias, her mother?

Herod was living. Herod was partying. Herod was enjoying himself, but not for long. Herod was about to be lost. His spiritual life had been on unstable ground for quite some time and each of his decisions, each of his actions, brought him closer to his spiritual death. Then it occurred.

The hushed silence of the palace party guests and the soft whispers moving from person to person were broken by the daughter who "came immediately to the King saying, 'I want you to give me at once the head of John the Baptist on a platter' " (Mark 6:25). Using her daughter, Herodias was going to get her way.

Herod was now exceedingly sorry. Herod suddenly and shockingly realized that he was really living between a rock and a hard place. Herod was about to become a crushed man. Herod was out of control, not able to think straight. He was fearful, unable to take a moral stand. Herod believed if he now took the road of doing what was right, he would disappoint the girl. If he chose to act morally and courageously and didn't honor the daughter's wish, he would go against his wife and family. If he reneged on his offer, he would make a fool of himself in front of all his guests. Changing his decision meant he would reveal himself as a party pooper and show his guests that he was a wimpy ruler who wouldn't keep promises and oaths.

Herod immediately sent a soldier of the guard to behead the Baptist. Satisfying his family and subjects, but failing to stand courageously for what was morally right, Herod sold his soul. Herod traded the Kingdom of God for the kingdom of earthly desires. Herod placed another person's selfish, immoral wish above John the Baptist's life. Therefore, on the day when Herod was celebrating the precious gift of life given to him by God, he took another's life. The result of his decision and action was his own spiritual death.

This is a great story in the life of one's faith. This story is life as we hear about it, see it, learn it, and live it, even in today's world. This story, of John the Baptist's moral stand, vividly displays to us how God wants us to live the abundant Kingdom life. John the Baptist stood courageously steadfast and never wavered in following the call of God to do what was right. He paid the ultimate cost of discipleship. Later, Jesus the Christ, being faithful to God as John had been, also sacrificed his life on a cross so that we might live.

The story reveals, through Herod's role, how our world and many persons within it can lead us to suffer our own spiritual death. This biblical passage is really about each one of us. The passage is about options we find before us daily. This passage is about the consequences of the decisions we continually make either for self, for others, or for God. Like John the Baptist and like Herod, we do have a choice. We have the choice to choose between the temporary life of this world's kingdom or the eternal life of God's kingdom. We can select to travel the road of good or take the road of evil. We can follow the path of the moral or follow the path of the immoral. We can journey the way of justice or settle for the way of injustice. We can live our life in a personal relationship with God, as John the Baptist did. We can be examples of integrity and courage. Yet, we can also sin and become like Herod and find ourselves caught between a rock and a hard place.

Like John, like Herod, like Herodias and their dancing daughter, God gives each of us the freedom to choose life or death. The choice you have is to live between a rock and a hard place and suffer spiritual death, or choose to be in relationship to God and receive God's ultimate gift of life eternal. What decision will you make?

Proper 11 • *Pentecost 9* • *Ordinary Time 16*

Surviving In A Cordless World

Mark 6:30-34, 53-56

The twelve had been called by Jesus to engage in an evangelistic mission. Jesus sent them out in pairs to towns and villages throughout the land. Our Lord charged them to carry out an all-inclusive ministry. The twelve were to preach repentance. They were given authority over unclean spirits. Their efforts found them casting out demons and anointing the ill and infirm with oil. Their ministry resulted in many people being made well and countless lives being greatly changed. These disciples had a demanding ministry. They worked long hours and often found their lives ridiculed and their efforts rejected. Yet they persisted.

Today's lesson is the account of the twelve returning to the base from which they had embarked on their journey. They have come home to report to Jesus all that they had done and taught. But they also have come back for something else. They were drained disciples — men who needed to be refreshed, renewed, replenished, and recharged for God's work.

Jesus knew firsthand, the great demands and immense consumption of energy God's mission and ministry required. Seeing the disciples' weariness, identifying with their exhaustion, Jesus said to them, "Come away to a deserted place all by yourselves and rest awhile" (Mark 6:31).

These most welcome and refreshing words, given by Jesus to the twelve centuries ago, are words equally welcome and refreshing for all God's people at all times. Yes, words welcome and refreshing for you. Who among you is not in need of renewal? Who among you would not benefit this very moment from God's recharging spirit replenishing your life with the energy of new joy and the confidence of new hope?

Like Jesus' disciples, have we not been called to an evangelistic mission? As God's people are we not meant to live the faith into which we ourselves were baptized? Our Lord calls us to conduct a ministry of caring, compassion, and change which is all inclusive. Jesus challenges us to go into the world and be faithful to God through the words we speak and the things we do. Answering God's call requires much of us. Following Christ will be tiring as well as stressful. Done properly, living our lives for Christ will place overwhelming demands on us and bring unprecedented weariness and exhaustion to our physical, emotional, and spiritual well being. Service to God is nothing short of sacrificial. Christ's life given on the cross clearly reveals this.

We who live today on the edge of a new millennium live in a much different and much more complicated world than Jesus' first followers. We live in a world that is often moving much faster than we are, and it's hard to keep up. We live in a world that pulls our lives in more than one direction at a time, often forcing us to go places and do things against our will. We live in a world where more is expected and demanded of us than we are often capable of doing. Sometimes we want simply to give up and quit. Haven't we all felt this way? We live in a world that finds itself overwhelmed with alternative lifestyles and questionable moral behavior, leaving us to make choices that are not always clear to us. We live in a world hell-bent on individualism where dependence upon and committed relationships to others are often suspect and rejected. Best described, we live in a cordless world, a world in which we, as people, have become detached from the very spiritual source which gives and assures us of life, eternal life! The ultimate challenge for each and every one of us today is the challenge of surviving in a cordless world.

Think about it! The moment you wake in the morning until you retire to bed at night your life is dictated by a cordless world. You clean your teeth with a cordless toothbrush. You shave at the sink or in the shower with a cordless shaver. Your life at home and at work functions on cordless appliances, cordless power tools, and cordless electronic cell phones and pagers. Cordless controls operate your entertainment centers; they open your garage doors, and grant access to your locked automobiles.

Actually the moment we are born, we ourselves become cordless persons. We are detached people. My wife and I recently became grandparents for the first time. My son shared with me the tremendous experience and feeling that came over him and our daughter-in-law in the hospital delivery room. He spoke of their personal partnership in the birth of their new daughter. This was a day filled with numerous emotional happenings. However, one great moment that remains special to my son is the moment he was given the opportunity to cut the umbilical cord, giving their new daughter life on her own. A simple snip of surgical scissors and our new granddaughter, God's new creation, became cordless.

When the umbilical cord is cut we each become cordless. Have you ever seen a power adaptor in today's electronics stores that plugs into the human navel? Yet, I ask you: How often in our cordless world have you believed you can live your life permanently separated and detached from other people and from God? We cannot survive apart from each other or apart from our creator. As newborns, as teens, as adolescents, mid-lifers, or seniors, whatever stage of life we are in, there is a need for us to have a connection with others for our physical and emotional needs of life. Likewise we need a connection to the God of our faith. This connection assures that we will receive spiritual strength and guidance for the church's mission and ministry we are called to carry out in Christ's name.

We all know what happens when we leave the cordless phones, tools, and appliances off their power bases. They become weak, powerless, and unable to do anything. God has given Jesus the Christ to this cordless world in which we live. God knew from the time he tried to find Adam and Eve hiding in the garden that we, as cordless persons, were going to need a power-charging base. God knew we would have to return to our spiritual beginnings to receive forgiveness and renewal, and be recharged for living and serving God and others.

How can you survive in a cordless world? How can you remain faithful to the God of your baptism? How can you become charged persons when you've lived so long in the same demanding, tiring, make-ends-meet, rut of a world? How can any and all of us become challenged and serious about the church's mission and ministry?

The answer is found in the simple verse of Jesus' words in the lesson today. Jesus witnesses your weary, worn-out lives and he knows the needs you have. Jesus first witnessed his weary, worn-out disciples returning to him long ago. Our Lord lived firsthand the same demands, the same rejection, the same ridicule, as well as the very things that we find ourselves living today. Jesus knows, identifies with, and fully understands how tiring and taxing your life can be living in the fast lane.

Jesus' advice to his first twelve disciples long ago is timeless advice for each of you this very day, wherever you find yourself to be and wherever your life seems to be going.

Jesus says to each of you, "Come away to a deserted place all by yourselves and rest awhile."

Somehow, we don't want to hear these words. We all have our excuses, do we not? We claim we don't have time to come away. We work two jobs. The weekends are our only chance to sleep in, do the household chores, go golfing and boating. We're busy people. So busy that in our modern world we aren't connecting anymore. We're like the cordless phone left indefinitely off its base. We can't communicate anymore. We're like the garage door opener that has lost its power. Our very access to people and God has been closed and we've shut out others and God from our lives. We're like the cordless toothbrush, left off its charging unit too long. Our lives like uncleaned teeth are stained with misery and sin, with anxiety and hopelessness, and we're left wondering if the tartar that has built up in our life will ever be removed.

We're like the lawn and basement power tools. We've used our lives and our lives have been used by others so much that we've forgotten the importance and necessity of reconnecting ourselves to that which physically, emotionally, and spiritually gives us renewed life.

We've become a drained world of detached people. We've become couples who don't connect with each other, parents who don't connect with their children, children who no longer connect with aging parents, friends and neighbors who don't connect with one another. As a cordless world we need so badly to connect with God through Jesus Christ.

The words of the ancient palmist, recorded in the Old Testament, offer this advice: "Be still and know that I am God" (Psalm 46:10).

God becomes best known to us in the quiet moments of prayer and through the dedicated periods of our devotional time. Our contact with God is as important as the cordless items we use daily that must have contact with their power source. Surviving in a cordless world means hearing and heeding the timeless advice of Jesus given centuries ago to the disciples: "Come away to a deserted place all by yourselves and rest awhile."

We ask: How does one come away from life's busy schedules and heavy demands? Perhaps we need to think back to the years of our youth. Years when we lived life freely. Remember the times with playmates. Carefree times, good times with friends on those hot, humid afternoons when we gathered beneath a towering shade tree.

Jesus said, "Unless you change and become like children you will never enter the kingdom of heaven" (Matthew 18:3).

Somehow, as children, life's important things mattered and there was always time for them.

I can see him today as clearly as I saw him on that serene summer evening many years ago as my car passed by on the highway. A boy perhaps six or seven years of age. He was sitting atop one of two pillars made of white brick. The pillars marked a long winding driveway that stretched from the highway to a modern home. The home was constructed of the same white brick and was surrounded by a spacious lawn. The young boy was looking west, to where the setting sun appeared to be floating like a giant bright red beach ball and touching the treetops of the distant wooded hills. Captivated by the scene before him, with his legs crossed and his chin supported by his two hands, this young boy seemed lost in deep thought. A short distance away sat a lawn tractor, its engine silent and mowing blades still. The fresh alleys of cut grass leading back to the house told the story.

This was the deserted place to which the boy had come to rest awhile. Here the lad was refreshing himself from the work that he had been given to do. Perhaps he was consuming the creative beauty of God in the world around him. Maybe his eyes were closed and in deep thought he was offering his own special prayer. Whatever the case, one certainty prevailed. This boy was renewing his strength and recharging his life.

We all grow older in life. We become immersed in our careers and self interests and goals we set, seek, and believe are so important for ourselves. Yet, by our baptism, we are God's people. We are persons called by Christ to live and serve in a cordless world. We are people needing to return to the power base from which we receive renewed strength, direction, and hope for Christ's mission and ministry. Perhaps your special spot is a pillar at the end of a driveway along the highway of life. Maybe your deserted place for rest is a basement workshop, a sewing room, a favorite chair, or a vacation retreat.

Whatever your place might be, isn't it time you revisited your special place? Isn't it time you reconnected yourself to God in preparation to serve others in Christ's name? God's strength awaits you. God's love and comfort, God's forgiveness and mercy are always abundant and available to you.

Hear and heed Jesus's words, "Come away to a deserted place all by yourselves and rest awhile."

These are the words of our Lord and they are your key to surviving in a cordless world.

Proper 12 • Pentecost 10 • Ordinary Time 17

Pulling Valves And Pushing Fish

John 6:1-21

The 1961 Pontiac was sharp, clean, and candy apple red. The engine was a 389 with a four-barrel carburetor. The interior of the vehicle was as stylish as the exterior. Cars had no plastic parts to speak of back then. The inside door panels were a mix of carpet, vinyl, and chrome. The dash board was aesthetically artistic in its design. When the doors were opened, colored courtesy lights lit several areas. This was my dream machine. This vehicle took my wife and me through our dating days, college years, and seminary semesters. This classic of cars was durable and dependable, day after day, year after year, mile after mile, oil change after oil change, and it ran like the wind.

Then, suddenly, at 120,000 miles, something went wrong. An engine noise surfaced. A loss of power was experienced. The engine heads and valves needed replaced. We couldn't afford another car. I didn't want to part with this one.

My father-in-law, who was a backyard mechanic of sorts, and I decided to make the repairs ourselves. We worked on it in the evenings when I had a week's vacation.

Having torn down the engine and reached the valves, I could sense my father-in-law was puzzled. His usual confidence and quick, unquestioned hands seemed to be hesitant. He admitted he wasn't sure about how to remove the valves from the engine block.

While pondering the situation, a friend dropped by whom I hadn't seen in over a year. Realizing our predicament, he made the comment that what we needed was a valve puller. This friend saw our dilemma. He, too, was a backyard mechanic. He had been through a repair like this earlier in his life and knew what could be done to meet the need. He offered his resource, an idea. Using pencil and paper, he drew a rough sketch of what a valve puller looked like.

My father-in-law, the genius he was, took the diagram, added his creativity, and with scraps of metal and a welding machine fashioned a homemade device. Half an hour later we were pulling valves.

Did you ever notice how life has a way of placing before us unintended obstacles? Things we don't count on. Difficult, disrupting circumstances that challenge not only ourselves, but also our very faithfulness to Christ and to God's work. Sometimes these situations, like the valves, seem impossible and without solution. We pray diligently but often wonder if our prayers are heard. And yet, there are those among us who, like my friend, are able to see something we haven't seen. These persons, with their knowledge and insight, rise to the occasion. They help us meet the complicated challenges life, at times, brings our way.

This is what occurred in the feeding of the 5,000. Having crossed the Sea of Galilee, Jesus and his disciples settled themselves on a mountain some distance from the water's edge. Seeking long-needed rest from the weary demands of his teaching and healing ministry, Jesus looked up and saw yet another multitude of people coming towards them. These persons were seeking Jesus, knowing that he could satisfy their spiritual hungers and thirsts. Since it was close to meal time, Jesus also saw in these persons their need for physical food.

The scene is set. We find Jesus and his disciples facing one of life's unintended obstacles and disrupting circumstances. A situation on which they hadn't counted had presented itself. Here was another dilemma at a time they were in need of rest. However, the needs of the people and the world were so great, and Jesus and his disciples found themselves facing another physical situation with spiritual implications. How could Jesus turn the people away? How could our Lord say no? He couldn't. But, the more important question was: How could this multitude of people be fed? Physically fed? Spiritually nurtured for life? There were no towns or villages nearby. Fast food restaurants didn't exist and there were no pizzerias that delivered.

Jesus directed a question to Philip about meeting these people's needs. The question came as a test of problem-solving. Jesus knew that Philip was originally from the area. He believed Philip would know where enough food could be obtained to feed the crowd.

Another surprise! Philip was of no help. He quickly told Jesus that the crowd was just too large. There was not enough money to buy even a small amount of food. The problem was most difficult. The situation was unexpected and Philip chose not to get involved.

We can't help but think that Philip represents us at times. Perhaps Philip believed the people should have thought about food before chasing after Jesus miles from any town. Philip is that part in us that gives up before even trying. Philip is that part in us that dwells upon the negatives and emphasizes the attitudes of apathy. Philip is that person in each of us who says the hungry have only themselves to blame.

But we must say, "Wait a minute," to the world's Philips. Doesn't God give us a mission and a ministry to address human need, to meet problems, to solve situations? Like my faither-in-law and me standing and staring at those engine valves, sometimes we are baffled at what to do next. Sometimes, like Philip, we respond that the task is too great and our resources too small. We conclude it can't be done. We regret we got ourselves into the situation in the first place. So we ignore the challenge. We run from the challenge. We simply refuse to see the challenge through. We give up before we begin.

But then, there are the Andrews of this world. Andrew saw the crowd approaching. Overhearing Christ's question, Andrew was like my friend who dropped by the garage that day. The dilemma, the problem, the situation stares us squarely in the face. Although solving a problem appears impossible, problems intrigue the world's Andrews, just like the valves waiting to be pulled intrigued my friend. Andrew was thinking. Andrew was standing next to Jesus in our story and beginning to imagine the possibilities. Andrew was looking to address the concern and meet the need to which Jesus had called his disciples' attention.

Andrew, like my friend, spoke up. Andrew said, in so many words, "There's a lad here with five barley loaves and two fish. They aren't much but they're something."

Thank God for the world's Andrews!

Perhaps. Just perhaps. Awe! Yes! Andrew saw in that boy and his sack lunch a resource. Andrew did something else, which Philip didn't. Andrew put his faith and his trust in Jesus. Friends, if God's work is to take place, we as Christ's disciples must put our resources and trust into the hands of Christ.

When we are willing and when we choose to do these things, then the miracles happen. Yes! Miracles happen even today. Miracles like pulling valves within minutes after hearing my friend describe and roughly sketch a valve puller. Miracles like Jesus and his disciples pushing fish to feed the multitude of 5,000 plus within minutes of Andrew showing his Lord the lad with the sack lunch.

How deeply our world, our nation, our states, our cities, our neighborhoods and, yes, our churches are in need of having Andrews in their midst. If we are to be about God's work, if we are to do God's work, Jesus needs each of us to be people with vision, the vision to see that even the smallest resource can bring about the greatest miracle. What is your vision regarding yourself, others, the future, your church?

Think about this lad with the sack lunch. He must have seemed so small, so insignificant, in the crowd of over 5,000 adults. Yet Andrew spotted him. The sack lunch must have first appeared as inconsequential, of no real use. However, placed in the hands of Christ, even the smallest amounts of what the lad had to offer effectively met life's greatest needs. The same can be true of what you have in your hands. Entrusted to Christ there's no telling what miracles are before us.

So often the answers we look for to solve life's difficulties are right in our midst. All we need are the eyes of faith like Andrew displayed. All we need is the willingness to share what we have in our hands with the hands of Christ. As the story shows, Christ has the power to take what we have and make it enough to meet our needs and the needs of others beyond the wildest of dreams. May the power of the living Christ grant clarity to our lives by giving us the eyes of faith, as he did Andrew, so that our needs may be met and we, as well, can help meet the needs of others.

Proper 13 • *Pentecost 11* • *Ordinary Time 18*

Beneath Life's Surface Scenes

John 6:24-35

Leaving the state highway and turning into the entrance of the large city park, the road winds its way past the public golf course on the left. A half mile or so beyond the golf course there is a small pulloff to the right. Here a grass-clothed access road, blocked by a chain, leads into the woods. Something interesting, special, and wonderful for all persons of all ages takes place along this wooded lane. One only needs to walk but a short distance down this path in winter and stop at the wood's edge to enjoy a most unique experience. Placing birdseed into an outstretched hand and extending an arm, chickadees and house finches will appear in the branches of the leafless trees nearby. Then, following a short period of patience, one by one, these fragile feathered creatures of God will take turns landing upon the hands that have come to feed them. These birds, in the midst of winter, through the efforts of park visitors, are provided with daily food necessary to sustain them in their physical life, while the rest of nature around them remains cold, harsh, and unrelenting.

Today's lesson describes for us a group of people, who, like the park birds, are experiencing the winter of their lives. They seek out Jesus that they, too, can receive something which is missing in their life. They have a need to be fed. These very individuals are those who saw, and heard about, and experienced the feeding of the 5,000 by the outstretched arms and hands of the one called Jesus. These persons have pursued Jesus by crossing the Sea of Galilee and entering the north shore village of Capernaum. Like the birds in the park woods, these followers of Jesus desired physical food. They were people with hungers and thirsts. They had sought Jesus knowing that he had fully demonstrated his ability to fill their empty stomachs. Yet filling their physical needs was not all that Jesus could or was willing to do for them. Although they were unaware of it, Jesus had the power and the blessing of God to feed their deep spiritual needs and cravings. Jesus had the power to turn sadness into joy, despair into hope, emptiness into fullness, brokenness into wholeness.

Having found Jesus, our Lord spoke to them saying, "Do not labor for the food which perishes, but for the food which endures to eternal life, which the Son of Man will give to you; for on him has God the Father set his seal" (John 6:27).

Here is God's complete and ultimate promise. Immediately we come to realize in this text that Jesus is at a deeper level of thinking than those who followed him across sea and land for food. Those persons had a limited view, a limited vision of the bread Jesus had to offer. Those who had left their homes and dropped what they had been doing to chase after Jesus all the way to Capernaum were completely caught up in the physical realm of life. They had neglected to consider the more important spiritual aspect of their life and living. Those who followed after Jesus had tunnel vision for the things of earth and hadn't yet begun to consider or acknowledge the things of heaven. When they saw the loaves of bread Jesus offered with his open hand and outstretched arms, these followers saw the loaves as common, ordinary bread. Jesus, however, in his ministry to their deepest needs, was offering them a chance to satisfy the stronger hungers and quench their more severe thirsts at a much deeper level than they could ever imagine.

Jesus, with his words and message, had led these hungering, empty persons to a place where they had never been before. Jesus was taking them beneath life's surface scenes. He was challenging them, encouraging them, and trying to help them realize that there is so much more to life and its living than simply meeting the needs of their physical appetites. His words are true. There is always much more to life and its living than accumulating things and storing up earthly goods. Jesus knew something they did not know. Jesus knew that even after these people ate their fill of bread, to the point where they could eat no more, even after they had consumed the very last crumb and pushed themselves away from the food-filled tables, they would leave those tables still unsatisfied. They would leave the tables still having the feeling of being empty inside. They would walk away from those tables still having hungers and thirsts that remained unmet.

So Jesus informed them, "Do not labor for the food which perishes, but for the food which endures to eternal life; which the Son of Man will give you, for on him has God the Father set his seal."

These challenging words given by Jesus to the people of his generation and world remain equally challenging and applicable to us who are living today. When we think about it we are really no different than those who sought after Jesus hoping to receive his gift of loaves of bread. We too, even in our lives of affluence, continue to hunger and thirst. We get ourselves all caught up in the pursuit and in the acquisition of the physical things of earth while we continue to neglect the pursuit of the spiritual things of heaven. Yet we are people with a soul. We have a spirit world deep within that seeks after God, a spirit that needs fed, a spirit that desires to foster a deepening relationship with the Holy One who has given us life.

However, we often become driven by a world that tries to convince us that we can physically have it all and be happy. We get caught up in the obsession for the food that perishes and we miss out on the spiritual food which endures to eternal life. This very food, the only food that can fully satisfy our need and longing for the relationship with God that is deeply a part of who we are and who we hope to become, is the spiritual food Christ offers. We find we are people who continue to hunger and thirst and feel empty even after having filled our lives with so much of the earth's bread. We are people, like those of Jesus' day, whose greatest need often remains unmet.

Our unmet need is to have Jesus take us to that place where we, in our lives, have never been. We need for Jesus to take us beneath life's surface scenes as he did those who followed him that day to Capernaum. We need Jesus to challenge us. We need Jesus to encourage us. We need Jesus to help us realize that there is more to life and its living than that which meets our physical appetites. We are also spiritual beings, people of God, who long for a relationship with God and others!

When one travels abroad to places beyond one's culture and home, there are many new things one sees and experiences. Having traveled to numerous countries and cultures abroad, I always come away with something unique and different from each journey, something which stands alone in the images of my mind.

A recent journey through Scotland proved no different. While there, we visited not only the larger cities of Glasgow and Edinburgh, but we had the unique opportunity to visit the Isles of Sky, Mull, and Iona. These were accessible only by ferry. We also spent several days on Loch Ness and Loch Lomand.

The word *loch* is an old Gaelic word for lake. The lochs of Scotland are a chain of narrow lakes that act like an outstretched arm that extends from the North Sea inland. These lochs or lakes connect and they feed and give life to the people and towns and villages that extend across the northwest section of Scotland's beautiful, heather-covered hill country.

Here in our ferry crossings and boat travels on these lochs, I was taken to a place I had never been before. The clarity of water enabled me to see for the first time what was beneath life's surface scenes of the lochs. Several times as the boats moved away from shore we could peer into the water of Scotland's lakes and see a world beneath the surface, a world that was clean and pure and active with a fullness of life. We could visualize rocks and plants and follow the pattern of fish swimming. If we viewed the lochs from a distance or across their surfaces, this entire life-giving world was totally missed. The lochs simply looked no different than average lakes.

The point to be made is that when we view life from only its surface or physical side we totally miss the life-giving spiritual side. Jesus the Christ calls each of us to a life beneath life's surface scenes. Jesus challenges us to look deeper into the life God has so richly blessed us with. Jesus wants for us to believe on him "for the bread of God is that which comes down from heaven and gives life to the world" (John 6:33).

The people who follow Jesus, we who listen to Jesus' words, "Do not work for the food that perishes, but for the food that endures to eternal life," need to trust completely in our Lord just as the park birds trust completely the outstretched hands that feed them daily in winter. Just as the birds come to the outstretched hands in the park to have their physical needs met, we have come today to the outstretched arms of Christ to have our spiritual needs met. God's seal is set upon Christ. God's seal is the validation, the promise to each and all of us that when we journey beneath life's surface scenes, when we labor for the food which endures to eternal life, we shall come to know Jesus like never before and have life in most fulfilling ways. Jesus' promise to each of us is this: "I am the bread of life; he who comes to me shall not hunger, and he who believes in me shall never thirst" (John 6:35).

May each and all of us leave here today knowing that Christ is the bread of life which can satisfy even our deepest hunger and thirst. May we also know that Christ is the bread which endures to eternity.

Proper 14 • *Pentecost 12* • *Ordinary Time 19*

Wearing the 7C6 Label

John 6:35, 41-51

I want to take you back to that time in your life when you made the transition from elementary school to junior high or middle school. The seventh grade was the transition period for me. I might add that it wasn't a very good one. Perhaps it can be said that moving from elementary school, up the ladder so to speak, to the next rung can be a difficult time for most young people. Suddenly your life is turned upside down. Remember? Back when I moved from the sixth grade to seventh, you left the elementary school behind. Elementary school was the place to which you walked from home, the place where you knew everyone and felt secure. This was where you had one teacher for each grade the entire year. This was where you brought the class cupcakes on your birthday and had parties for Halloween and other significant occasions, and life was good.

Remember entering seventh grade when it all changed overnight? Suddenly at 7:15 in the morning, you're on a bus traveling far from home to a bigger school across town where other busses arrived and you knew very few students. Suddenly you found yourself with six different teachers and only six minutes to get from one classroom in the great building to the next classroom. If you were late that was a crime. You received a prison sentence called detention or were given corporal punishment with the paddle.

If this weren't bad enough, there was gym class. Remember gym class? That new experience where you were forced to take showers with everyone you didn't know or like and you had to be naked. I never knew what a shower was because all our home ever had was a bath tub.

Then there was that dreadful thing that marked you, sometimes for life — acne! And no matter what celebrity advertised them or how tremendous they sounded, the miracle creams never worked. To make things worse, your parents told you that you couldn't eat chocolate or greasy pizza anymore.

It was a tough life and tough times. But worse than all this, worse than the label of acne or the label of peer pressure or the adjustments to all the changes occurring was wearing the academic labels. Remember those? The labels established by all the tests you took. The tests where you filled in all those tiny circles on the answer sheet with a number two yellow lead pencil. Tests, where the results told you who and what you were.

Lumped together in my homeroom were the 7C6s. This meant we were just average. The 7C1s were the A students who took all the accelerated and advanced classes. They were college bound, always a unit or two ahead of the rest. There were also the 7C10s. They were considered the problem ones. The ones that the teachers spoke about saying, "Oh no, you mean they have younger brothers and sisters? How many? How old?"

Seriously. Think about this. The importance of these labels, or any labels we are given in our growing and maturing years, is that once they are placed upon us or once we place a label upon another person, they stick. They stick like price tags in today's discount department stores. Label remover might easily take off the store price stickers, but labels placed on people permanently remain.

The labels of students are limiting; the labeling of any person is limiting. Labels put us in categories that aren't always correct or don't reflect our capabilities. Labels inhibit growth and advancement. Labels define who we are and what we do, and often prevent us from striving to be anything else than what others have defined us. Labeling is universal to all and is often a negative fact of life.

This is exactly what happened to Jesus. Having grown and matured in life, Jesus had accomplished many good things for God.

His ministry was sound and his mission had been productive. He had credibility in his God-called efforts. From the time he was twelve and was found by his parents to be in the temple, as Luke relates it, Jesus "increased in wisdom and in years and in divine and human favor" (Luke 2:52).

However, Jesus was given a label to wear by those who had known him way back when. Jesus was stuck with a label that he could not shake off, overcome, or change. We can accurately assume that the words of the scripture text are words spoken by individuals who knew Jesus in his younger growing up years. These were individuals who unfairly labeled him and could see him no differently than he was in his early life. They said, "Is not this Jesus, the son of Joseph, whose father and mother we know? How can he now say, 'I have come down from heaven'?" (John 6:42).

Those who unfairly labeled Jesus with these words of bias and prejudice put Jesus in a box. These persons had seen Jesus as a child, watched him grow up, and observed him through his teens and adolescent years. Now, sometime later as an adult, they saw him the same way. They refused to admit Jesus had changed. Jesus for them was, is, and always would be Joseph and Mary's son. Jesus, for them, was the kid who played on their street, ran through their yards, and raided their gardens and olive trees. Jesus, for them, was the one who got into mischief with the other kids on the block. Jesus was the one who hung around his father's woodshop and took over when Joseph died to help support his mother in the raising of his siblings. Jesus was the local boy who never excelled in school and never spent a day in seminary and wasn't very refined in his ways.

This is the label those in the text have slapped upon Jesus. They couldn't accept and they refused to accept Jesus' claim that he had come down from heaven. The Pharisees believed Jesus and his work couldn't be of God.

Do you realize that each and every one of us, at times, can be like these ones who labeled Jesus? We actually do refuse to believe that Jesus' work and ministry are of God. Like these persons, we also label people. We, too, refuse to believe. The result is we greatly limit our possibilities and our living. Do we not also greatly limit the possibilities and living of others?

There are some things that are so hard for us to understand and to accept, just like moving from elementary to junior high or middle school. One of the most recent and difficult advances in our lives today, which many of us find hard to understand, is this thing called cloning. We say to ourselves, "How can this be?" One part of us wants to deny that it has happened. We don't want to believe it. We aren't sure what to think of it. We're at the place where science has out-paced ethics. We wonder: Is it right or wrong? We wonder: Is it of God and what does God think?

The first cloning, as you know, took place in Scotland. The first animal cloned was a sheep. On a recent trip to the United Kingdom, I heard the story about the scientist who cloned a parrot that had an extreme gift of gab, but couldn't fly. The scientist lived on the tenth floor of an apartment building and kept this cloned parrot as a pet. One night the scientist went to bed and forgot to turn off his television set. The after-midnight programming was totally adult in content. The shows simply were filled with all sorts of adult situations, both spoken and seen. The cloned parrot, who couldn't fly, picked up several hours of worthless vulgarities.

The next morning, the parrot was out of control. The parrot began shouting loud profanities and inappropriate descriptions of what it had heard and viewed on television throughout the night. The scientist was beside himself. He couldn't get the bird to be quiet. What would the neighbors think? What could he do? Finally in an act of anger and desperation, the scientist grabbed the cloned parrot. Forgetting he couldn't fly, the scientist tossed the bird out the tenth floor apartment window. The cloned parrot, of course, fell to the street below and died.

People passing by thought such action horrible and became involved. They called the police and demanded the scientist be charged with the crime of murder. The police, lawyers, and judges considered charges of murder, but found no law on the books to charge the scientist for a parrot's murder. Finally they did charge the scientist. You will never guess with what crime he was charged. He was taken to court for making an obscene clone fall.

Now you can believe this story or you might choose not to believe it. Whatever you choose to do, the point of the story is exactly this: Belief. Your belief and my belief in Jesus the Christ. How do you see Jesus? These ones who knew Jesus as Joseph and Mary's son, they who labeled Jesus based on observing our Lord's earlier life, could not and would not believe that Jesus was the bread who came down from heaven. They could not accept Jesus as being from God because they had unfairly attached their labels to him. They could not accept that Jesus was the perfect image of God sent to redeem the world. Those who knew Jesus were unwilling and unable to believe that Jesus could offer them the very life they so desperately lacked and needed. Tragically they missed out.

Is this not a problem within our lives today as well? Will you, because of unbelief, tragically miss out on the redemption and the gift of life Jesus offers simply because you can't believe who Jesus is? We, too, unfairly label Jesus. We label Jesus as one we heard about in church school but, having grown older, feel we no longer need to believe in or follow. The result is we fail to realize Jesus has the fullness of life we lack and desperately want to receive.

We label Jesus today as simply being a nice guy, a good teacher. We forget what's most important: He is the "bread of God which has come down from heaven."

The New Testament message which winds itself through the Gospels, the Epistles, and even the book of Revelation is the message that God has come to the world and comes to us in Jesus the Christ. This message is like a single strand of thread in a garment making the garment whole and complete. Christ is the thread who can make your life, once and for all, whole and complete.

We, like those of Jesus' day, label Jesus and for us the label sticks. Our unfair labels limit what Jesus can do in our eyes. Our unfair labels limit the life we could have for ourselves. Our labeling of other persons is also life limiting, to them and to us. Our labeling also limits what's most important of all: the very mission and ministry of Christ's Church addressing the needs of the world, society, and people's lives.

There is a great prejudice and injustice revealed in this text. There was prejudice and injustice against Jesus. There was prejudice and injustice in school when you were given academic labels. There is also prejudice and injustice in each of our lives when we label, categorize, or judge other persons because of who they are, where they have come from, and our knowing something about their prior life circumstances.

God speaks to each of us through Jesus. We can be taught by God if we are open to hear and, most importantly, if we are open to learn. God has been speaking to the world through Jesus for centuries. Yet, as John's Gospel reveals, "The world did not know him. He came to what was his own and his own people did not accept him. But to all who received him, who believed in his name, he gave power to become children of God" (John 1:10b-12). Jesus still gives power for you to become God's children if you will remain open to him.

The message of Christ today is for us to take off all the labels which breed prejudice and injustice in our lives and in the lives of others we know and have known. The message is that we must once and for all remove all the labels that limit, hinder, confine, and keep us and others from being all that God has expected.

When we can do this, we shall more clearly see God's purpose in our life. When we can do this, God's true servants will be revealed to us in all their completeness. We will be very surprised who God's servants living among us are. They will be those we knew in school. They will be 7C1s, 7C6s, and 7C10s. When we remove the labels of people we shall see Jesus and others in a new light, even as bread come down from heaven. May you feed upon the Christ, the true bread of heaven, and may God's gift of eternal life be yours.

Proper 15 • Pentecost 13 • Ordinary Time 20

Beyond The Oak Table

John 6:51-58

The day is picture perfect. The scene is a park lake, clean and tranquil. The lake draws to itself children, youth, and adults. They come to fish. They come to watch the ducks that float on the water's surface.

A young boy stands at the edge of the lake with a mission in mind. His mission is to feed the ducks. Reaching into a bread bag, the boy removes a slice of bread. Using his arm and the flick of his wrist, the boy sends the slice of bread sailing like a Frisbee across the lake's surface. When it hits the water a nearby duck is observed going for it. However, what happens next greatly surprises the viewer.

The scene drastically changes. Instead of the duck devouring the slice of bread, what occurs is quite unusual and extraordinary. That piece of bread speedily sails through the air, returning to the boy, from where it originally had come! The boy, who first threw that bread, is seen standing in shock with a wide open mouth and eyes as big as saucers.

This clever commercial advertising a local bakery offers a very clear and concise message. The message is: There's a big difference between the bakery's own brand of bread and the bread of all its competitors. So big a difference in fact that even hungering ducks on a tranquil park lake know the difference. They know the difference so well that they refuse to eat the inferior bread and send it back, knowing it will not satisfy.

Like the television commercial which emphasizes that differences exist in bread, Jesus, long ago, emphasized the differences in bread. Bread for all of us is a staple of life. Bread is important and necessary and essential. Bread provides the building blocks of life. Bread sustains us in life. Jesus makes it quite clear that there is the living bread from God which comes down from heaven, bread that brings us eternal life. Jesus also informs us that there is the bread of the earth which the fathers ate and died.

The point of Jesus in this passage is that life for each and every one of us is much more than mere earthly existence. Life goes beyond our simply moving through the motions of daily waking, eating, working, and sleeping. Life has much more to offer than our being born, living our given time, and dying. Yet how many of us live in such a way? The good news is that true life and true living, as God has meant for it to be, can only be fully realized when we are able to form a devoted and dedicated relationship with God and with one another.

This is the point behind the lesson where Jesus refers to himself as the living bread, the bread that leads to eternal life. Jesus' message is that all breads of the world give temporary satisfaction. Jesus, however, is the bread that satisfies forever, for he is the one who fosters our relationship to God.

Most significant about this lesson from John is the fact that the words *life*, *live*, and *living* appear eleven times in the eight verses. There can be no doubt that Jesus wants us to know that what is most important is that fullness of life, completeness of life, and meaningfulness of life are more than just meager existing. Jesus is saying that to have a relationship to God who promises the true gifts of life we first must have a part of Jesus himself. Jesus, as the living bread, is connected to God from whom we receive life abundantly when we have part of him. Therefore, when we are connected to Christ we, too, are connected to God in a meaningful, life-giving, life-sustaining, life-receiving relationship.

Jesus proclaims that one must eat his flesh and drink his blood to receive this eternal life. What Jesus is saying here, metaphorically, is that we need to receive him totally into our life and living. We must take Jesus into ourselves so that his words and his deeds become a part of us. Jesus is saying to each of us, "Feed on me, receive me into your hearts, and minds, and souls. Be filled and saturated with my example of complete humanness; receive my blood, the very symbol of God's gift of life itself."

If your life seems to be out of synchronization for you, if your life appears to be missing something, should you find yourself or your life lacking excitement, purpose, fulfillment, my question of you would be: "When was the last time you fed upon Christ?" When did you last read his words, hear his teachings, heed his examples? We can't help but be challenged by Jesus' words to take Christ unto and into ourselves. Should we really want life to be fulfilling we must be challenged to make him the very center of who we are, what we wish to be, so that we become the person God created us to become.

The bread on our tables is that which builds physical bodies. This bread nurtures and gives us energy by which to live. The earth's bread also satisfies our hunger pains until we hunger again.

But Jesus is the living bread, the bread which satisfies forever. Jesus, as the living bread, builds our relationship with God, nurtures the energy of our faith living, and satisfies us completely so that we shall never spiritually hunger again.

Fully receiving Christ, the living bread, means we must not limit or confine our relationship to God at the communion table or at the altar in the sanctuary. Receiving the abundant life, the complete life, and the meaningful eternal life God promises means we must go beyond the sanctuary's oak tables upon which the sacrament of Christ's living bread is found, offered, and received into ourselves.

Having received the living bread of Christ we must take the living bread to others in the world. The breakfast, lunch, and dinner table in every home is to be a table for Christ and an opportunity for sharing the living bread. Whenever bread is broken, shared, and received at a table in a restaurant or banquet hall or at the shore of a park lake, those tables like the tables in our homes and churches need to be places where Christ is present and always remembered. Every table needs to become the place where Christ's presence prevails. Each of your lives must be nourished by Christ the living bread.

In our devotion and our dedication to God, we must feed our starving world the living bread of Christ through our example of mission and ministry. Therefore, may the spirit of the living God challenge us to eat of the living bread of Christ, and drink of the cup of Christ beyond the oak table of the sanctuary. For as Jesus has promised, those who have part in him shall receive eternal life.

Proper 16 • *Pentecost 14* • *Ordinary Time 21*

The Raft Of Passage

John 6:56-69

Anchored a fair distance off the shore of the great lake called Erie, it was constructed of planks of lumber supported by fifty-gallon metal drums. There it loomed, for some in a haunting way. This floating platform captured the attention of children on shore; it was a goal every young person dreamed of reaching. It was the focus much talked about by the youth who visited the vacation spot each summer. Those who were approaching adolescence viewed this floating gathering place for youth as an historical site. This simple platform had played an important role in the lives of countless youth who, over the years, swam to it, dived from it, and rested upon its surface before making the return swim to shore.

Swimming to the platform was the test of every young person, male or female, who aspired to be someone. This is where recognition was received by those who braved the depths of Erie's waters and swam the distance from shore to the raft. This was where one was judged by one's peers to be worthy of group acceptance. When a swimmer reached the raft for the first time, immediate cheers were received from those who had previously accomplished such a feat. This raft was where one passed from childhood to adulthood, from being "no one" to being "someone." This raft was the raft of passage.

The time had arrived for yet another young person to be tested. He had watched for several years as those older and more experienced at swimming made the journey. He had heard the cheers as others lifted themselves from the threatening waters onto the raft.

He had witnessed the warm reception received, the acceptance displayed through back slapping and the giving of high fives bestowed on those who successfully completed the swim. He contemplated the thought of his reaching the raft and being able to say the "Yes!" of personal victory. Now, having spent several days at the lake, he began to believe this was his summer, the summer he would join others of the elite group on the raft of passage.

Slipping into the dark water, deeper than his own height, he began the crossing as others watched from the raft and on shore. All was going well. He had the strength. He had the endurance for the swim. He covered better than three-fourths of the distance. Yet something happened within him. He began to wonder if he would reach the raft. Suddenly his confidence started to waver. His swimming began to slow. He believed the distance yet to swim was too great. He drew back. He turned away from the course which he had earlier determined to complete at all cost. Swimming away from the raft he kicked wildly, covering at least twice the distance he had already traveled. He sought a place where he could solidly plant his feet on the lake's sandy bottom. Having deserted his cause, all he could do was disappointedly stand on shore and hope that some day he would reach the raft of passage.

The young boy had turned away. He had lost what he had gained. He had chosen the course of least resistance. His decision to turn back on this important test and goal diminished his self-esteem and withered his spirit. He decided the goal wasn't worth the sacrifice. He again became a settler on the shore and gave up joining the pioneers on the raft of passage. Yet, all the while, his return to shore was unnecessary. Should he have chosen to stay the course, he would have easily reached the raft.

There is also, for each of us as persons of faith, a raft of passage. Such a raft plays a significant role in the life of every single one of us. As God's people, we enter the waters of our baptism and embark on the journey which takes us across the sea of our life. This raft of passage captures the attention of all God's people. This raft of passage is much talked about by the followers of Jesus Christ. This raft of passage is God's eternal life, the realm to which we each aspire. It is the realm where our lives shall be judged by God to see if we have been faithful in fulfilling the mandate of Jesus Christ.

Jesus spoke of this raft of passage for God's people when he taught in the synagogue at Capernaum. He referred to himself as the bread of life. He challenged others to feed upon him so that they might live. He specifically laid down not suggestions for faithful living, but necessary principles each of us must follow if we are to receive spirit and life.

The young adolescents at the lake contemplated from shore how and when they would set out for the goal of Erie's raft of passage. Similarly, we as God's people come to hear, to see, to accept, and to follow Jesus' words, teachings, and actions. Our faithfulness to God and to Christ requires us to keep our attention fixed upon and our efforts committed to reaching the goals of mission and ministry which God places before us.

The text tells us that many of Jesus' disciples, when they heard his teaching, said, "This teaching is difficult; who can accept it?" (John 6:60). And Jesus knew from the first who those were that did not believe and who it was that would betray him. And Jesus knows you and me better than we know ourselves.

The text also states: "Because of this, many of his disciples turned back and no longer went about with him. So Jesus asked the twelve, 'Do you also wish to go away?' " (John 6:66-67).

By our parents' faith or by our own faith, we have entered the waters of baptism. Through communion we have been fed and nourished upon the flesh and blood of Christ. We know what is good and what the Lord requires of us is "but to do justice and to love kindness and to walk humbly with your God" (Micah 6:8). And we know these are hard sayings to live by and put into practice. Jesus' teachings are God's call to us to engage in mission and ministry, and we, like Jesus' first disciples, ask, "Who can accept it?" The challenges Jesus places before us are not easy. Meeting such challenges will require us to endure all that life and its living places before us. Such endurance will only occur if we allow the Spirit of the living God to have first priority in our lives.

Many of us, like Jesus' first disciples, and like the boy in the midst of his swim to the raft, turn back from life when it becomes difficult. Many of us decide that continuing across the waters of our baptism toward eternal life in Christ is much different and demands much more than we first anticipated or believed. We find the claims of Jesus require more than we at times want to sacrifice. We discover that the faith walk for Christ and with Christ asks more of us than we are willing to give. We can endure our faith walk with Christ by realizing that we need the comfort, the strength, and the support of the church, God's community of faith, to strengthen and encourage us along the journey.

Jesus' question to his twelve closest disciples in the lesson today is Jesus' very question to each of us today. Realizing that multitudes who start to embark toward the raft of passage, for whatever reason, turn away, Jesus asks us, "Do you also wish to go away?" What of you? And you? And you?

Here it is, plain and simple. The test of our faithfulness doesn't get any clearer or any more specific than this. Jesus asks you the question, and Jesus gives you the choice. Will you also leave? Will you abandon the cause, retreat from the goal of the Holy One? Will you give up the quest for eternal life? Or, will you stay the course and become a part of the Saints of God and join the great crowd of witnesses that have gone before you?

Consider for a moment the importance of Jesus' words, "Do you also wish to go away?" Friends, this is not a question Jesus asks at our baptism. We want to be baptized and we want our children to be baptized. This is not a question Jesus places before us when we stand at the front of the church to be received into membership. Like the swimmers, we want to belong. This is not an inquiry Jesus raises on those occasions when we share the gifts of bread and wine at the table of our Lord's supper. We find it easy to partake of the bread and drink of the cup in a peaceful sanctuary. "Do you also wish to go away?" This is Jesus' question regarding the life-making decisions with which we are confronted every hour of every day. This is Jesus' question when you find yourself in the midst of the swim when the outcome is unclear. This is Jesus' question when your faith's strength begins to weaken and your commitment endurance begins to fade. This is Jesus' question when the current of life's sea is pushing against your every effort to glorify God in your living. "Do you also wish to go away?" is Jesus's question when the waters of life's challenges descend on you like a flood and the tides of injustice threaten to swallow you up in all your God-directed endeavors. This is Jesus' question to which we, in unwavering faithfulness to God, need to stand firm and answer with the conviction of Peter. Peter was so confident that when he answered Jesus, he answered not only for himself but for others: "Lord to whom can we go? You have the words of eternal life. We have come to believe and know that you are the Holy One of God" (John 6:68). Peter, in order to endure, gave himself over to Jesus. Peter, in order to receive the support of Christ and the support of God's people, fully trusted in his Lord and placed his entire faith in the all encompassing power of God's community. There was no question in Peter's mind. He faithfully reached the raft of passage.

Looming in the distance for each and every one of us is God's raft of passage. It's out there. We've seen it from where we find ourselves safely on shore. Biblical history proves to us that it is the gathering place for all who are God's faithful people, youth and aged, male and female, wealthy and poor, regardless of one's skin color, racial differences, or ethnic diversity. God's raft of passage captures the attention of children who learn of it in church school. It's a goal much talked about by those whose dream is to some day reach it. The raft of passage is where God calls each of us to eternal life. We know of the ancestors who have gone before us. They endured the journey because they had unwavering belief that the struggles of the journey were worth their efforts. They endured the journey because they had unwavering faith that Jesus would enter the waters and travel the journey with them. This raft of passage is where we come to the realization that once we were not a people, but now we are God's people. Likewise, once we had not received mercy, but now we have received mercy.

The raft of passage for people of faith is out there across the great sea of life. The sea contains unknown challenges and harbors great mysteries and darkness in its depths. The sea offers not just sunny skies and serene surfaces, but unstable rolling clouds and storm-delivered mountains of water. The crossing of the sea of life tests our faithfulness levels. The God who calls us takes us through the waters of our baptism and leads us into committed Christian service toward the raft of passage. God, therefore, is not a distant God who stands on the shore of life refusing to enter the sea's turbulent waters. The God of our faith is the one who walks with us through the waters of calm and storm. This God is the one who grants us strength for the tasks and endurance for the journey. God offers these things through God's Spirit, as well as through the blessings, the commitments, and the presence of others in the faith community.

Therefore, it is in the midst of the swim to the raft of passage that Jesus comes to each of us and asks, "Do you also wish to go away?" Each of us faces and will continue to face this question throughout our lives. Life's journey is never simple or easy or without blemish of sin. Life is tough. Life tests us, and passing the test means we will need to use resources God has placed before us, resources of the faith community, the Holy Spirit's presence in our midst, and the openness of a God who will not turn us away or abandon us in the midst of the swim. Therefore, should Jesus come and ask in the midst of the swim, "Do you also wish to go away?" what will be your answer? Will you be like the swimmer who failed to proceed and out of uncertainty turned back, or will you be like Peter who said with confidence, "Lord, to whom can we go? You have the words of eternal life."

Proper 17 • *Pentecost 15* • *Ordinary Time 22*

Hey, Don't Ruin The Bean Pot!

Mark 7:1-8, 14-15, 21-23

There was a time, long ago, when families had just one car and when all the children gathered at the one house on the block that had the only television. This was a simpler time. A time when a computer took up several floors of an entire building and virtual pets hadn't been born. This was a time when an exceptional amount of creative spirit and energy came from children who constantly congregated along the curb at the street corner. A time when the Cleaver and Nelson families were the norm and Father always knew best.

I recall one afternoon when Joey showed up after lunch. He carried a small instrument called a magnifying glass. Magnifying glasses can be quite magnificent, you know. In a short time we were doing all sorts of things with that magnifying glass. We turned tiny bugs into tremendous beasts. We observed the hairs on the back of a cat. We looked closely at petals of flowers and studied the veins of leaves. This got to be so popular that before you knew it, we all carried magnifying glasses. We either brought them from our homes or purchased them with our allowances at the local Woolworth's store.

Somehow we came to discover that getting the sun to shine through the magnifying glass produced an awesome power. Tilting the glass just right and moving it toward or away from an object harnessed the energy of light. The circle of light created by the sun's rays passing through the magnifying glass became like a laser which we used to cut holes in leaves and sticks and to burn our names in baseball bats. One boy burned holes in his US Keds.

We all thought it was great; however, we soon discovered his parent's didn't appreciate it at all.

The scripture verses from Mark come to us today like the separate rays of the sun. The verses are scattered throughout the first half of chapter seven of Mark's Gospel. This being the case, I want to challenge you to use your mind as if it were a magnifying glass. I ask you to bring together and to concentrate on the common central theme these scattered verses create. When you do this you will discover a very precise picture of a faith-related issue that has crossed the centuries. The issue was brought to light by the ancient prophet Isaiah. The issue is dealt with by Jesus in today's text. The same issue also presents itself to us who live at the threshold of a new century. This extremely ancient, yet also contemporary, issue is about a struggle in the life of each and every one of us. This is the struggle we have of attempting to live a life which follows the will of God.

The lesson begins with the Pharisees and scribes gathered around Jesus. These religious leaders of the time had not come to greet Jesus graciously. They didn't show up to inquire about how his ministry was going nor to acknowledge the tremendous good he had done for others. These religious men had come with pointed fingers. They had come with an agenda to criticize. They sought to discredit our Lord. They couldn't wait to tell Jesus what they had seen! Jesus' disciples had eaten without washing their hands. God forbid!

Now it is very important for us to know that the handwashing these religious leaders were confronting Jesus about was not handwashing as we might perceive it or engage in it today. People of Jesus' time didn't often wash their hands before eating. Handwashing was not done for hygienic reasons or to comply with the universal health standards. What these religious leaders were confronting Jesus about was that his disciples did not obey the intricate, detailed rules and laws of religious ceremonial handwashing. Simply put, the disciples had neglected tradition. They had failed to carry out what had become the all-important externals of religious policy and procedure.

This had nothing to do with obeying the will of God. This, in fact, was what Jesus saw and addressed as the entire problem of his time and culture. The people's faith practice was no longer based on living the commandments of loving God and loving their neighbors. The people's faith practice had become a complicated nightmare of trying day and night to follow thousands of trivial traditions. People actually believed this was the way of doing God's will.

This is seen in the passage which adds, "and there are also many other traditions that they observe, the washing of cups, pots, and bronze kettles" (Mark 7:4b).

True, the disciples may have been eating with defiled hands, but as Jesus pointed out the religious leaders were living with defiled hearts.

Have you ever been to a New England bean supper? Bean suppers are a New England tradition which are exactly what one imagines. Everyone brings a pot of beans. Sounds really appetizing, doesn't it? Kind of like attending a broccoli bake-off. However, let me continue. Each recipe is distinctly different in taste and flavor. What makes this so is each individual bean pot. When corn bread is added and the supper is concluded with a piece of apple pie and a slice of cheese to top it off, you've had a meal!

One evening my wife and I were invited to dinner at a friend's house. This life-long resident of Maine had a pot of beans as part of the dinner. They were fantastic! The best beans I'd ever eaten.

Later as my wife helped wash the dishes, while vigorously scrubbing deep into the bottom of the bean pot, our hostess blurted out, "Hey! Don't ruin the bean pot!" What she meant by this was quite simple.

The bean pot was an antique that had been in the family for over a hundred years. This glazed, surface-cracked pot had been used by this woman's great-great-grandmother for her beans and by every mother since. The bean pot was like a seasoned iron skillet, a family heirloom. The stains, along with its crusty bottom and color differences, were permanent. Vigorously scrubbing and scouring it might result in breakage. The pot might become too clean. The inner heart of the pot which produced its unique family taste and flavor of beans might become forever destroyed. You see, it wasn't so much what went into this bean pot that mattered. What counted was the magical, almost mystical flavor that came out of this bean pot. That's what made it so very special.

This is what Jesus was basically saying to the Pharisees when they asked him about the disciples not washing their hands. Realizing how caught up in external religious rituals the Pharisees had become, Jesus said, "It's not what goes into one's body that counts but what comes out of one's heart." Jesus' words could easily have been, "Hey, don't ruin the bean pot!" In other words, don't make God's kingdom and love less than it is. Jesus was making it known that the religious leaders' passionate pursuit of ceremonial cleanliness was hindering their faith life. Their obsession with washing hands, cups, pots, bronze kettles, and just about everything else had become a real problem. A real faith-hindering problem. Their engaging in thousands of other trivial traditions had destroyed the people's ability to follow the commandments of God properly. No longer were they involved in loving others.

Jesus told them exactly how it was, using Isaiah's words, "This people honors me with their lips but their hearts are far from me" (Mark 7: 6b).

Isn't it interesting? The problem that Isaiah and Jesus identified in people thousands of years ago remains the very same problem we have today. We, too, honor God with our lips while many times our hearts remain far from God. We, too, magnify rules and hold to traditions that aren't easy for us to give up. These same rules and hard to change or let go of traditions many times prevent us from being about and doing the very thing God calls upon us to do.

Jesus makes very clear what's most important if we are to have a healthy relationship to God and others. He says what matters most is not the external activity of what we do, like cleaning bean pots. What does matter most, however, is what comes forth from the inside of our heart.

We live in a world in some ways not much different than the world of Isaiah and Jesus. We, like the people of their time, are a people seeking and searching to be more spiritual. We honor God with our lips, and yet what we all seem to miss and really want is to have our hearts closer to God.

Jesus made an extremely profound statement for all persons of all times when he said, "The kingdom of God is within you." Repeat these words with me, "The kingdom of God is within you."

The point Jesus was making is that our spiritual relationship with God begins from deep inside our hearts. Our deeper, more spiritual relationship to God will come about only after we individually realize that change is needed. Not external change as the Pharisees and scribes tried to bring with all their washing rituals. Not change in those people different than us who we want to conform to our way of thinking and doing things. Change is needed within us. Internal change that takes place in the deepest part of our hearts. Your heart is the source of your spirituality. Your relationship and my relationship to God is simply a matter of the spirit and not a matter of our following a list of do's and don'ts. Approaching life and God in any other way other than through the Spirit tends to ruin the bean pot.

If I may take you back to the illustration of the magnifying glass for a moment, only after we were able to get the heart of the glass correctly positioned and properly focused on objects could we see clearly the wonders God's world had to reveal. Likewise, for each of us, it is only after we are able to get our hearts spiritually positioned and focused on God that we will be able to live faithfully according to God's will. When God is first in your hearts, God will be first in your life. When God is first in your life, then your every word and action will flow from your heart to others. When you allow God to become first, above all else, you will not only find the spiritual richness your life has been seeking, but you will discover the kingdom of God in your midst as Jesus proclaims and promises. And when that kingdom is discovered in your midst, life will become focused and God's will shall be clearly seen.

Proper 18 • *Pentecost 16* • *Ordinary Time 23*

Who Are You?

Mark 7:24-37

Beginning in late fall, throughout the winter months, until the first signs of spring, Grandma always had a picture puzzle going. The puzzle pieces occupied the surface of a card table in an out of the way corner of the living room. Grandma had boxes upon boxes of puzzles. They were stacked along the stairs which led to the attic. Once worked and returned to their boxes Grandma would trade them with family and friends for different puzzles. Overnight stays at Grandma's usually meant putting pieces into the puzzle. Sometimes we would finish one. This meant experiencing the joy of dropping the final piece into place and making the picture complete.

I recall one particular puzzle that we finished. Grandma was preparing dinner in the kitchen and the final pieces were quickly coming together. I picked up the last puzzle piece from the table top and attempted to place it in the one empty spot that remained. The color seemed right. The size and shape were similar but the puzzle piece didn't fit nor belong.

We all at times in our individual lives encounter situations, experiences, and people that, like that one last puzzle piece, seem out of place and just don't belong.

This story of the puzzle piece not fitting came to mind as I read, reread, struggled with, and actually agonized over this particular scripture lesson. The lesson describes for us a brief dialogue between Jesus and a woman. The woman sought Jesus out to receive help for her demon-possessed daughter. Like that puzzle piece, the lesson today shows us a side of Jesus that doesn't seem to fit. We have a portrait of Jesus who is acting differently than the Jesus Mark has been describing since the beginning of his Gospel.

Mark's presentation of Jesus to us is a Jesus who is very human. Mark's account shows us that Jesus, like us, is baptized and faces temptation as we do. Jesus, like us, gathers people together and makes himself accessible to people. He is a teacher of wisdom and a person of warmth and openness. Jesus, as Mark has been describing him, is rejected at times, but also is bigger than life. Mark's Jesus is one who walks on water and brings healing and wholeness to people who suffer illness and brokenness in their lives.

Based upon Mark's Gospel, we believe we know Jesus. Yet, seven verses of our text today suddenly reveal to us a Jesus who doesn't fit into the picture we're used to seeing.

We actually are left puzzled and we are forced to ask regarding Jesus, "Who are you?"

Jesus, in the lesson, went away from the region and from the people he knew so well. Jesus stayed in a home and didn't want anyone to know he was there. Jesus entered Gentile territory in a very secretive way. Jesus almost seemed to be engaged in a role reversal with Nicodemus. Nicodemus, you'll recall, came to Jesus by night so those Nicodemus knew wouldn't see him associating with Jesus.

Mark also gives us a very negative, demeaning picture of the woman who has chosen to seek Jesus out. She is a Gentile, a non-Jew, a pagan. She's a Greek woman from the part of Syria known as Phoenicia. More startling is that Jesus identifies her not as a person but as a dog, the lowest creature of society. This woman came seeking help for her demon-possessed daughter and Jesus responded to her in a rather harsh way. This story of healing reveals to us a Jesus who appears extremely uncaring and prejudicial.

The story leaves us shocked and asking Jesus: "Who are you? Who have you become?"

The Jesus in this healing story is the piece of a puzzle that doesn't seem to fit.

However, this woman of tremendous faith who sought Jesus' help does not argue with Jesus over his considering her a dog. Rather, she engages in a dialogue that proves very interesting.

Paraphrased, Jesus tells her after she begs for his help that the children (meaning the chosen people of God) must be fed first. Therefore, it's not fair for him to take the food of God's people and give it to persons like her who are seen as dogs.

This woman basically replies, "What you say, Jesus, is true. I have no right to expect anything. I'm not a privileged person. None of us are, but even dogs eat the children's crumbs which fall under the table."

What the woman is telling Jesus is that she doesn't want a whole loaf of the bread Jesus offers to his own people. She doesn't even want a whole slice or half a slice for that matter. The woman is simply asking and begging for Jesus' permission to have a chance to retrieve a crumb from such bread that falls to the floor.

Here is a woman who believes strongly and deeply in Jesus. Here is a woman who has a complete confidence and faith in the Lord, a woman who knows that a mere crumb of Jesus' love, a small scrap of his healing power, a minute amount of his leftover compassion will be more than enough to save her daughter. The woman has no doubt that a remnant piece of what Jesus brings from God shall deliver her daughter from the awful demon that has possessed and tormented her young life.

Here, at this very place in the story, God acts and brings a change to Jesus. Here God refashions the shape and changes the size of a puzzle piece that, up to this time, does not fit into the picture of God's making.

How do we know this? We know this because suddenly Jesus sees this woman as a child of God. Suddenly, Jesus permits her to go home. When the woman does, she discovers the demon gone from her daughter.

This unusual story forces us all to ask ourselves the question: Who is this Jesus who first treats the Gentile woman so differently than we have come to expect? The answer we receive is that Jesus, in this particular story, reveals himself to be a person much like ourselves. Mark gives us a very human Jesus. Jesus at this stage of his ministry is struggling, as we often struggle. He is attempting to discover who he is in relationship to God. He is trying to keep intact his loyalty to who he is, taking into account his culture, his people, his upbringing, and the traditions he's been taught. However, in God's sight, Jesus had room to grow and his ministry was also growing. And grow they did!

The good news is that we also have room to grow and we also are growing in God's sight. Mark uses this story of Jesus to show all the world, including us, that the gifts of mission and ministry of God are not given to or for a few choice persons, but are for all God's children.

Often times we say things in the name of God and the church that lead people to say, "Who are you?" Meeting the woman's need shows each of us that just as Jesus grew in faith and expanded his mission and ministry to others, we too must be open and do the same. Sometimes we say and do things which later cause us and others to wonder who we really are. Isn't it time we face up to who we are as God's children?

As the story shows, there is a part in all of us that wants to run away from people. We want to escape responsibilities and not tell others where we can be found. There is a part in each of us that wants to keep our faith to ourselves, neatly nestled inside the walls of our local churches. There is a part of us that is prejudiced and so we place all sorts of blame on people different from us. We create all kinds of excuses why we should not or cannot reach out and ease the pain or meet the needs of others. We rationalize why we at times ignore the empty souls and empty spirits of God's people. Others ask of us and we also are left asking ourselves, "Who are you?"

The good news of God, as we worship in this time and at this place, is that there is hope for each and all of us. There is a place for the size, the shape, the color, the style, and the beautiful variety of gifts that make each of us a special, needed piece of the total picture of God's unfolding kingdom within our midst.

The last week of August and the beginning week of September, 1997, will remain forever indelibly etched upon the hearts, minds, and souls of people everywhere. We all know where we were and what we were doing when we learned the shocking news of the tragic death of Diana, Princess of Wales and Princess of the world. We all know where we were and what we were doing when several days later we experienced more sadness when we heard about the death of Mother Teresa, a mother to our modern world. One walked the marbled halls of Kensington Palace and one walked the filth-littered streets of Calcutta, India. One was tall, vibrant, and young from a circle of great wealth and royalty. One was short, frail, and aged from the squalor of the world's worst poverty. Yet, both their lives were touched by the call of God that asked, "Who are you?" God helped both Princess Diana and Mother Teresa grow in faith and serve the diseased, the afflicted, the downtrodden, the outcasts, the maimed and broken of the world. These two lives were pieces of the puzzle of life that will forever reflect the love and the beauty, the commitment and the compassion of God's most faithful servants.

We too are God's puzzle pieces that, at times, just don't seem to fit or belong. We think things, we say things, and we often do things that are so different from what people and God know and hope for us to be. Yet, as the story of the scripture reveals, there is hope for all of us.

Back at Grandma's house that day so very long ago, I took the puzzle piece that didn't fit. I went into the kitchen and told Grandma it was the only piece left and it didn't fit. Grandma went to the mantle over the fireplace. She knew something which I was about to discover.

She picked up another puzzle piece that rested there and said, "Try this one."

The piece wasn't too much different in shape, size, or color than the other. However, it was changed enough so that, like magic, it smoothly dropped into place. The puzzle was now complete. The emptiness in the picture was filled and the scene that had been gradually coming into focus for weeks was now whole.

God's love changed Jesus over the years and he grew and faithfully fulfilled God's will. God's love can change any life in so many different and special ways, even yours. Once you allow God to touch your life, the puzzle and picture of your life will become clearer and more complete. Once God touches you, you shall be able to reach out with your life and, like magic, add so much to the lives of others around you.

Unlike Diana, Princess of Wales, you may never have wealth and royalty to share. Unlike Mother Teresa of Calcutta, you may never experience doing ministry in the squalor of great poverty. Yet, you can grow in faith and serve God wherever you find yourself in life. You can do good work. Always remember, every time you touch another person with your faith, every time you help meet a need, another person is healed. There is reason to rejoice. You can rejoice because what you have done has resulted in there being one less demon loose within God's world.

Proper 19 • *Pentecost 17* • *Ordinary Time 24*

The Fine Print

Mark 8:27-38

Congratulations! **You've Won!** Your mailbox; my mailbox; hundred of thousands of mailboxes across America are bursting with personalized proclamations declaring we are all winners. Computers, entertainment centers, mountain vacation homes, sports utility vehicles, cruises, and trips to exotic islands are just waiting for us to claim them. All we need to do is call the toll-free number or sign and return the post card.

Sounds perfect. Seems easy. But, what have we actually won? What, in reality, is there for us to gain? Does sacrificing virtually nothing win us a free trip to life's multitude of magic kingdoms? I know a couple whose middle school aged daughter got off the school bus one afternoon. She grabbed up the mail as she always did, and was overtaken by a wonderful announcement that the family was the winner of a trip to the Bahamas. Believing the message and reading that a response was needed immediately, the young girl made the call and excitedly claimed the prize before her parents arrived home from work.

As it turned out what was won was not a prize, but a good lesson in philosophy. The philosophy that if something seems to good to be true, it most certainly contains obligations and commitments of which we were not aware.

Most of us know that in the space between the enticing bold-lettered announcement proclaiming we've won and the bottom of the page, where you put your name on the dotted line, there appears an often gray area called the fine print, the specific details. The sentences and paragraphs of disclaimers that make it quite clear that in this lifetime there are no free lunches.

Such details bring us to the realization that beyond the hype of the personalized letters, the wonderful phone calls, and the well-marked brochures and pages of promotional pleasantries, there are sacrifices to be made. There are expectations to be met and, yes, often a cost to be incurred. There is fine print for everything and it appears on virtually everything. The fine print always speaks up front and close about the commitment that's required.

Mark's Gospel according to biblical literary scholars is the earliest of the recorded written Gospels.

The author of this life and times account of Jesus and his ministry introduces us to Jesus at the moment he is called into ministry. We are told Jesus is baptized by John, that he receives the Holy Spirit, and has his calling and ministry endorsed by God. The author of Mark then methodically moves us along, showing us a Jesus who works through his own personal experiences of temptation and chooses who will be his first disciples.

Then begins the actual work of God. Engaged in an itinerant ministry Jesus walks the lands of Galilee healing the ill, preaching to those who are eager to listen, and teaching many persons about God.

Certainly, for the earliest of his disciples and for those who had the privilege of hearing, seeing, and experiencing the work of Jesus, life was good, refreshing, and exciting, to say the least.

Many must have been deeply moved when hearing and experiencing firsthand Jesus' storytelling through parables. Many must have been impressed and awed as they witnessed the powerful change in people, the results of Jesus performing his many miracles. Imagine then, Jesus' disciples. These early followers had a front row, reserved, box seat. The were the inner circle.

There had to have been a wonderful feeling in these followers as they embarked upon new adventures with Jesus. The disciples must have been experiencing some great moments — the refreshing "aha" moments we all have known the first few days and weeks of those new adventures to which we have been called and have favorably responded. The feeling is something like opening that fancy letter in the mailbox. Reading in our innocent naivete the big bold letter proclaiming the message **Congratulations! You've**

Won! The best part is you didn't even register. Oh, how easily we are led into believing how good life can be. How easy and simple it appears to be at times.

This lesson from Mark finds Jesus and the disciples traveling through the villages of Caesarea Phillippi. Jesus realizes that now is the time for him to help the disciples move to their next level in their spiritual growth and development. Jesus knows that he must help his followers visualize the reality of participatory ministry versus a spectator ministry.

Friends, we are called by God to a ministry where we get our hands dirty versus one where it's all handed to us on a silver platter. The disciples have responded to God's call. The bonding process has been occurring. Now, the time has arrived when Jesus believes he must assess where the disciples are in their faith thinking process.

He generalizes his approach with the disciples by beginning with the question, "Who do people say I am?" (Mark 8:27). Then he personalizes the question, asking the disciples, "But who do you say that I am?" (8:29). Jesus met the disciples on and at their level. Once he establishes where the disciples' understanding of ministry is, Jesus then introduces them to a more mature understanding of ministry. He proceeds to tell them what it means for him to be the Messiah. Jesus tells his disciples and the crowd that true discipleship is more than listening to parables and witnessing miracles.

It is important for each of us to know that Jesus also has a way of meeting us where we are. Jesus informs all who would be his followers that true discipleship involves sacrifice. Fulfilling mission and ministry involve a cost. The joy of discipleship is an important outgrowth of the cost of discipleship.

Somewhere between hearing and learning of the kingdom of God and being an active advocate for the kingdom of God lies the fine print. The fine print of self-sacrifice. The fine print of denying ourselves. The fine print of taking up a cross. The fine print of losing life as we know it, expect it, and often want it in order to gain the life God hopes for us to live.

Perhaps the greatest word in Mark's Gospel that we all need to hear, the words that refer to the fine print of Jesus' way with us, are the words, "He said all this quite openly" (8:32). Are we not a society and a world which is desperately in need of openness? As we leave a millennium behind and head into a future looking for promises and for hope and for God, the act of passing across can't be achieved with closed doors. There is no hidden agenda with Jesus. There must never be attempts by ourselves to hide the fact that the gospel of Christ calls us to be up front, honest, and open. To do otherwise is only to experience a part of what God offers. The fine print of Christian service is never hidden by Jesus to be sprung upon us by surprise. We on the other hand must always be open to the fine print offered, given, and shared by Jesus. Being counted among the faithful of Christ's followers, being true to answering God's call, and responding to Christ with complete commitment, we too must accept the fine print that accompanies the call.

The fine print for the true followers of Christ goes beyond worship attendance. The fine print in faith living calls us to overcome our complacency. The fine print means we do more than simply come to the church. The fine print challenges us to engage in ministry beyond the church doors in the wider areas of our daily living.

Jesus called the crowd along with his disciples in this lesson. He informed them of the important specifics of the fine print. Jesus told them up front and personally what it means and what it costs to follow him. Jesus made it clear the fine print is for all, not just the twelve, not just the clergy and the church staff or those installed at the annual meeting. The message of the fine print is that human thinking and human actions must give way to divine thinking and divine deeds in each of us.

Are we not the crowd being called by Jesus today? Do we not all hear, see, and experience what others say about Christ? The important questions must always be: Who is Christ to you? Who is Christ to me? Who is this Christ to each of us in the here and now as we struggle with making practical, moral, and spiritual choices? These choices we make will affect not simply our own lives, but the lives of all God's children who are an important part of the human family.

Jesus' message for our generation, as we move into the new millennium, is a message that calls us to serve others through self-sacrifice. Jesus equally challenges us to live fully. Jesus calls us to follow him in our daily walk so that our life example fosters excellence in serving God.

Jesus, by his own life, has proven that the joys of discipleship are experienced only as a result of our accepting the cost of discipleship first. Jesus by his own example shows how being faithful to God can move us and others beyond being human, to experiencing the blessed wonders and goals of God's divine will.

The fine print is found in our gospel living just as it is found in all of life. Make no mistake. The fine print, spoken quite openly by Jesus, does involve a cost. We need to be forever aware that failing to accept the cost of discipleship means that we also forfeit and miss out on the many joys of discipleship.

The question we all must ask and ultimately answer is: How willing are we to pay the price? The medal-winning Olympian knows the ultimate feeling of joy as the national anthem is played and the flag of his country is raised. It's a great moment of achievement. It's a blessed reward to have reached what seemed at various times an unattainable goal. Yet the athlete also knows the cost involved, having endured the long hours, many months, and often years of training. As the athlete sacrifices much in the training process just for the privilege of competing, we too as followers of Christ must always remember God's call requires us to sacrifice much. Again, the joy of discipleship only comes after we have endured the cost of discipleship. The way to Easter joy and to Easter living is not reached by taking the easy street. Easter joy and Easter living is fully experienced only after we have traveled the difficult road of self-sacrifice through the hill country of Good Friday. Jesus not only said this quite openly but he also lived it quite openly. Will you as Christ's followers be inclined to do the same?

Proper 20 • Pentecost 18 • Ordinary Time 25

Focus

Mark 9:30-37

A recent visit to the ophthalmologist became quite an eye-opening experience. Signs and images had been a problem for some time. The thorough exam revealed that the prescription lens, allowing vision at a distance to be improved, needed strengthened. New glasses were ordered. When they arrived I was thrilled. The thrill was short-lived. When I put the glasses on, the clarity of distant vision improved immediately. However, there was a downside. Everything within six feet was a blur. Reading while wearing the new glasses was virtually impossible. In discussing this uncomfortable dilemma with the physician, it became evident the difficulty in this situation was strictly a matter of focus. No longer were my eyes able to focus on objects near and far through lenses designed for one kind of visual need.

The scriptural text also has to do with vision. The text speaks of the kind of focus we must have if we are to remain faithful to the call of God upon our lives. The text describes the position Christ asks us to take if we are to remain true to the mission and ministry of God.

The setting of the lesson finds Jesus passing through Galilee with the disciples. Jesus was trying to travel in a discreet way. He didn't want anyone to know his travel route or his agenda. Jesus was attempting to use this private time to teach his disciples about his pending suffering, death, and resurrection. This wasn't the first time Jesus tried to explain what the call to follow God involved.

In the preceding verses of this particular chapter of Mark, Jesus has been to the mountain top with Peter, James, and John. Through the transfiguration experience, God has given the disciples a portrait of Jesus as the beloved son. That portrait revealed Jesus as the one to whom the disciples and each of us need to listen. Jesus is the one example we must follow as the people of God. Jesus is the one we are to focus on in our faith response to God. Our Lord's purpose and calling to be a servant to all was explained to his followers several times. He had spoken to the disciples before and after the transfiguration. His conversation with them was about God's intention for his life and theirs. Now on the journey to Capernaum, he tries to get his disciples to understand the servant-role of living for God. Jesus is attempting to emphasize that serving God is not about who will be the greatest. However, the disciples didn't get it. As the text reveals, "They did not understand what he was saying and were afraid to ask him" (Mark 9:32).

We, too, often misunderstand Jesus' servant principle. The lens God hopes we all would view life through is not ground or made in a way that allows us to have life both ways. The same optical lens can't be used to correct nearsightedness and farsightedness. Similarly, we can't concentrate on serving others when our efforts and energies are selfishly concentrated on establishing our own greatness.

The problem Jesus had with his first disciples is the problem we are facing today. We, like the disciples, love transfiguration-like events that take us to pedestal heights. We enjoy the special privileges, which often come with power, prestige, and social status. Yet, these special privileges often bring about an attitude of exclusiveness of others instead of the spirit of inclusiveness, which Jesus fostered. This is what led to the disciples' debating and arguing about who among them was the greatest.

Like the disciples, we don't understand Christ's servant principle. Our mind's eye is blurred to Jesus' teaching about his Messiahship. Often our intentions to follow Christ are good. We believe we are faithful, well meaning, and active Christians. We struggle over our Mondays through Fridays, working hard every week. We visit our places of worship seeking to be ministered to but forgetting that we are called to minister to others. We like being served and having our needs catered to and met. Like Jesus' disciples, we cherish most those things that best serve us. However, Christ calls us to a life of service. Duty and responsibility, reality and necessity call us back to the stations of our lives. The benediction and postlude after worship signal that our service for God hasn't ended but is about to begin. When worship concludes, we walk through the church parking lot. We enter our vehicles and direct our cars and our energies back to the real world.

Did you ever notice how we always return to the real world where we are to be a Christ-like presence to others? Yet somewhere between our sanctuary worship and our Sunday lunch the vision of serving God becomes distorted. The clarity of what God wants versus what we want becomes blurred. The joy of tranquil worship settings and spiritual highs begin to fade. The world shows us things and asks us to do things that are not in keeping with the mandate of Jesus Christ. Certainly being a servant is not as exciting as holding positions of popularity, power, social status, and greatness. Being the greatest is much more appealing than being second best.

The choice to abandon the call of God often is made because the call of God requires us to give instead of receive. We abandon the call of God because God's call is often unpopular. Let's be honest: Jesus' agenda is not a fashionable agenda. Living for God requires focus! Our complete focus! We have a God who is clearly focused on us. We have a Lord whose sacrificial love was focused toward us. However, like the disciples, we fail to see this clearly. We are like those persons who put on a new pair of glasses for the first time. We expect everything to be perfectly clear at all distances, but we find our lives terribly out of focus. The ministry and mission of God's kingdom remains blurred only because it is impossible for us to engage in selfish pursuits to achieve greatness and be a servant of Christ at the same time.

In the text Jesus is talking about how serving others requires sacrifice. The disciples, however, are oblivious to his words. They are involved in arguing about their status, their position, and their own levels of greatness. The issue for the disciples is not one of knowing or not knowing what the Lord requires. The Lord has told them. The question wasn't did the disciples believe or not believe? The disciples knew what the Lord required and they deeply believed in God. Like the disciples, we also know what the Lord requires and we also deeply believe in God.

The issue for us isn't an absence of faith or having insignificant amounts of faith. The issue for us is that we choose to ignore the words of Christ who explains what it means to be his servants. More and more we are conforming to a world which emphasizes a "me first" philosophy of life.

Our passion for pursuing personal greatness and achieving positions of social status has become stronger than our passion for serving others and standing firm for social consciousness. We have continually expected to be served by others, instead of following the Christ who, by his own example, shows that we are to be serving others.

Again, focus is the key. Focus is everything. Entering the twenty-first century, as followers of Jesus Christ we must do more than simply state what we believe about God. We must undergo a transformation and accept a new vision as Christ's servant church. Our focus needs to go beyond what others consider greatness to understanding what the word of God defines as greatness. Our focus as Christ's followers must discern God's will, so we can effectively live doing God's will in the new era.

As the opthalmologist adds a lens to correct and give us brighter, clearer vision, Jesus placed a child into the midst of his disciples. Jesus, through the child, demonstrated that the focus of faithful mission and ministry must never be about personal greatness, prestige, power, or selfish pursuits. The focus of faithful mission and ministry must always be about humbleness, innocence, and serving others. What is most important as we enter a new era in our world and in our own lives is: How will we live for God and Christ? The image of the child gives us a sense of new hope. The child illustrates there will be a future. However, God's vision for us and God's vision for others will only become clear when we focus on Christ as Lord. Then and only then, shall we come to understand fully that if we want to be first we must be last of all and servant of all.

Lectionary Preaching After Pentecost

Virtually all pastors who make use of the sermons in this book will find their worship life and planning shaped by one of two lectionary series. Most mainline Protestant denominations, along with clergy of the Roman Catholic Church, have now approved — either for provisional or official use — the three-year Revised Common (Consensus) Lectionary. This family of denominations includes United Methodist, Presbyterian, United Church of Christ and Disciples of Christ. Recently the ELCA division of Lutheranism also began following the Revised Common Lectionary. This change has been reflected in the headings and scripture listings with each sermon in this book.

Roman Catholics and Lutheran divisions other than ELCA follow their own three-year cycle of texts. While there are divergences between the Revised Common and Roman Catholic/Lutheran systems, the gospel texts show striking parallels, with few text selections evidencing significant differences. Nearly all the gospel texts included in this book will, therefore, be applicable to worship and preaching planning for clergy following either lectionary.

A significant divergence does occur, however, in the method by which specific gospel texts are assigned to specific calendar days. The Revised Common and Roman Catholic Lectionaries accomplish this by counting backwards from Christ the King (Last Sunday after Pentecost), discarding "extra" texts from the front of the list: Lutherans (not using the Revised Common Lectionary) follow the opposite pattern, counting forward from The Holy Trinity, discarding "extra" texts at the end of the list.

The following index will aid the user of this book in matching the correct text to the correct Sunday during the Pentecost portion of the church year.

(Fixed dates do not pertain to Lutheran Lectionary)

Fixed Date Lectionaries *Revised Common (including ELCA)* *and Roman Catholic*	**Lutheran Lectionary** *Lutheran*
The Day of Pentecost	The Day of Pentecost
The Holy Trinity	The Holy Trinity
May 29-June 4 — Proper 4, Ordinary Time 9	Pentecost 2
June 5-11 — Proper 5, Ordinary Time 10	Pentecost 3
June 12-18 — Proper 6, Ordinary Time 11	Pentecost 4
June 19-25 — Proper 7, Ordinary Time 12	Pentecost 5

June 26-July 2 — Proper 8, Ordinary Time 13	Pentecost 6
July 3-9 — Proper 9, Ordinary Time 14	Pentecost 7
July 10-16 — Proper 10, Ordinary Time 15	Pentecost 8
July 17-23 — Proper 11, Ordinary Time 16	Pentecost 9
July 24-30 — Proper 12, Ordinary Time 17	Pentecost 10
July 31-Aug. 6 — Proper 13, Ordinary Time 18	Pentecost 11
Aug. 7-13 — Proper 14, Ordinary Time 19	Pentecost 12
Aug. 14-20 — Proper 15, Ordinary Time 20	Pentecost 13
Aug. 21-27 — Proper 16, Ordinary Time 21	Pentecost 14
Aug. 28-Sept. 3 — Proper 17, Ordinary Time 22	Pentecost 15
Sept. 4-10 — Proper 18, Ordinary Time 23	Pentecost 16
Sept. 11-17 — Proper 19, Ordinary Time 24	Pentecost 17
Sept. 18-24 — Proper 20, Ordinary Time 25	Pentecost 18
Sept. 25-Oct. 1 — Proper 21, Ordinary Time 26	Pentecost 19
Oct. 2-8 — Proper 22, Ordinary Time 27	Pentecost 20
Oct. 9-15 — Proper 23, Ordinary Time 28	Pentecost 21
Oct. 16-22 — Proper 24, Ordinary Time 29	Pentecost 22
Oct. 23-29 — Proper 25, Ordinary Time 30	Pentecost 23
Oct. 30-Nov. 5 — Proper 26, Ordinary Time 31	Pentecost 24
Nov. 6-12 — Proper 27, Ordinary Time 32	Pentecost 25
Nov. 13-19 — Proper 28, Ordinary Time 33	Pentecost 26 Pentecost 27
Nov. 20-26 — Christ the King	Christ the King

Reformation Day (or last Sunday in October) is October 31 (Revised Common, Lutheran)

All Saints' Day (or first Sunday in November) is November 1 (Revised Common, Lutheran, Roman Catholic)

Books In This Cycle B Series

GOSPEL SET

A God For This World
Sermons for Advent/Christmas/Epiphany
Maurice A. Fetty

The Culture Of Disbelief
Sermons For Lent/Easter
Donna E. Schaper

The Advocate
Sermons For Sundays After Pentecost (First Third)
Ron Lavin

Surviving In A Cordless World
Sermons For Sundays After Pentecost (Middle Third)
Lawrence H. Craig

Against The Grain — Words For A Politically Incorrect Church
Sermons For Sundays After Pentecost (Last Third)
Steven E. Albertin

FIRST LESSON SET

Defining Moments
Sermons For Advent/Christmas/Epiphany
William L. Self

From This Day Forward
Sermons For Lent/Easter
Paul W. Kummer

Out From The Ordinary
Sermons For Sundays After Pentecost (First Third)
Gary L. Carver

Wearing The Wind
Sermons For Sundays After Pentecost (Middle Third)
Stephen M. Crotts

Out Of The Whirlwind
Sermons For Sundays After Pentecost (Last Third)
John A. Stroman

SECOND LESSON SET

Humming Till The Music Returns
Sermons For Advent/Christmas/Epiphany
Wayne Brouwer

Ashes To Ascension
Sermons For Lent/Easter
John A. Stroman